FOLDING STEPS

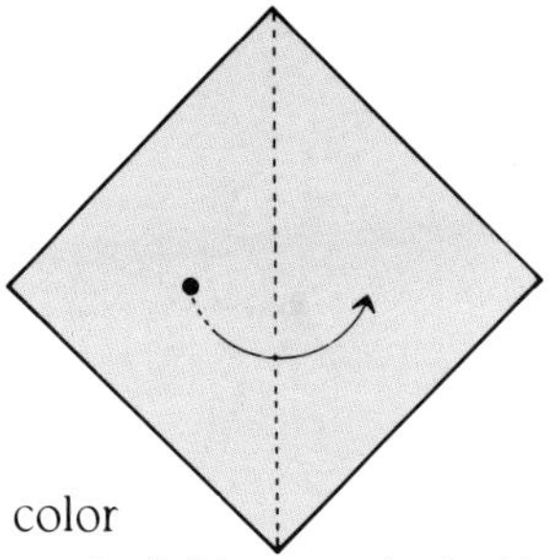

1. Keep color inside and fold paper in half.

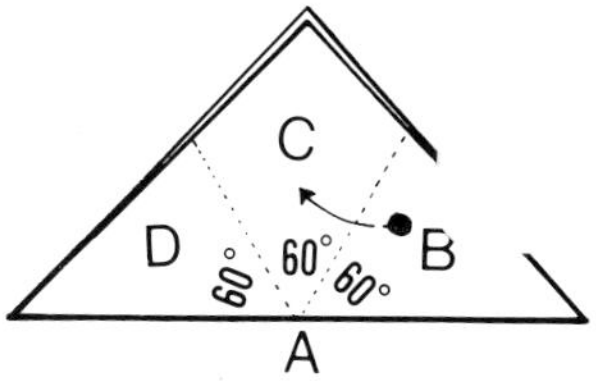

2. Use A as the center and fold B to C (becomes E) Keep ∠A-1, ∠A-2, ∠A-3=60°

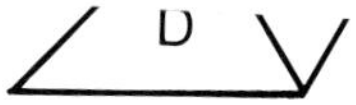

3. Fold D to E.

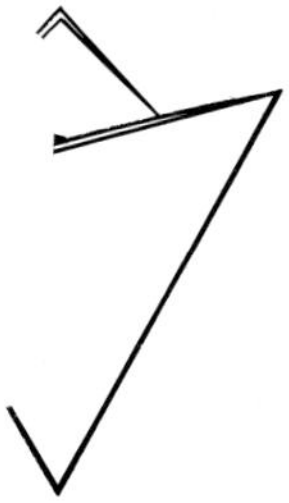

4. Ready for your design or follow pattern below.

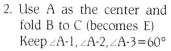

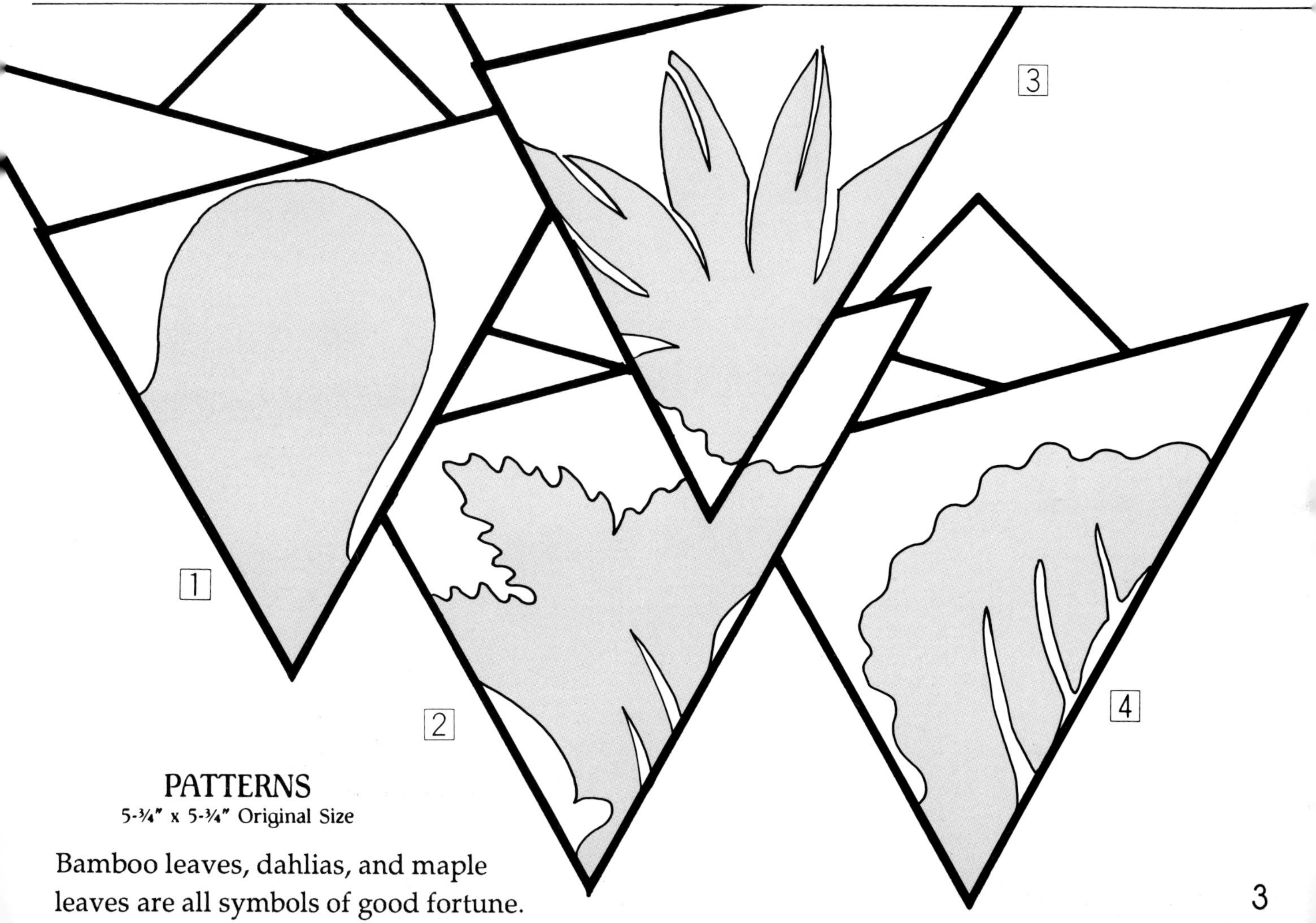

PATTERNS

5-¾″ x 5-¾″ Original Size

Bamboo leaves, dahlias, and maple leaves are all symbols of good fortune.

1 2
3 4

JADE

FOLDING STEPS

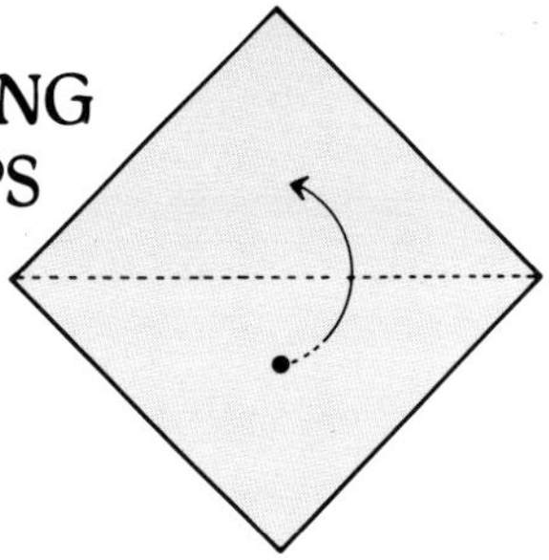

1. Keep color inside and fold paper in half.

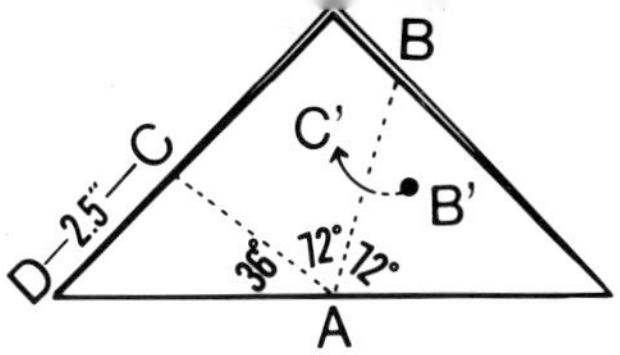

2. Use A as the center and fold B' to C'. For paper 5-¾"x5-¾", keep 2.5 inches between D & C. For other sizes of paper, keep ∠A-1=72°, ∠A2=72°, ∠A-3=36°. Fold as illustrated.

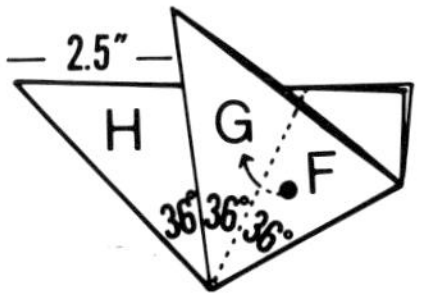

3. Fold F to G becomes I. Make sure that F, G & H have the same angle (36°)

4. Fold I to H.

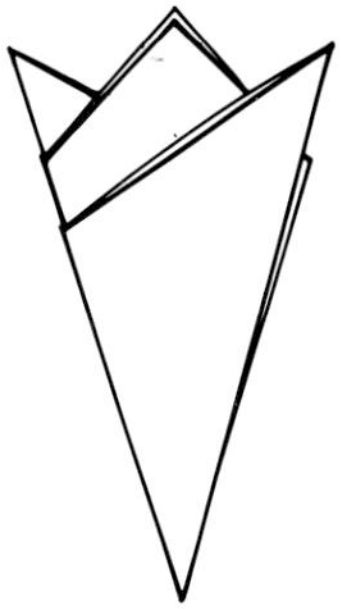

5. Ready for your design or follow pattern below.

PATTERNS

5-¾" x 5-¾" Original Size

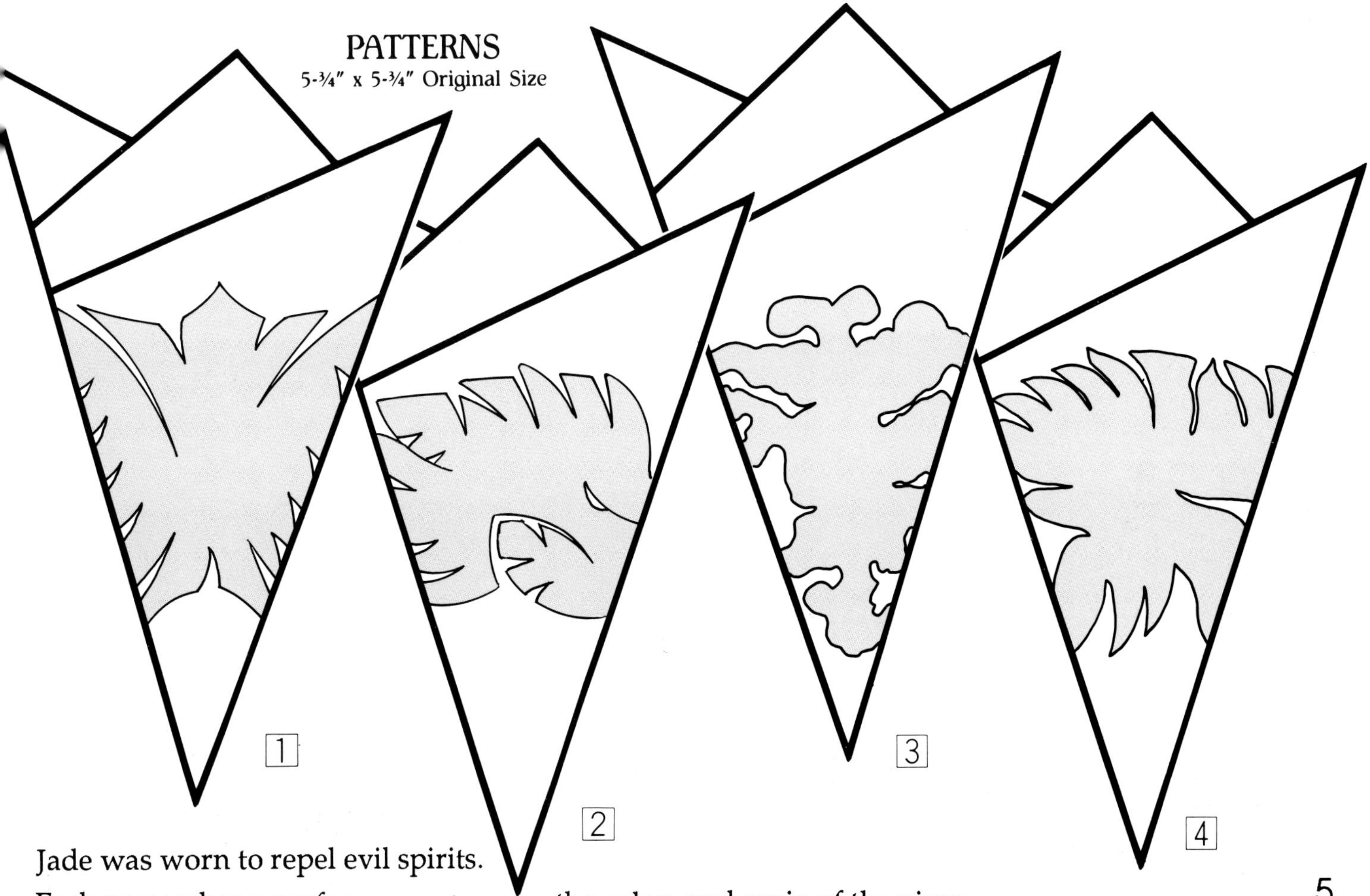

1 2 3 4

Jade was worn to repel evil spirits. Each person has a preference as to the color and grain of the piece.

1 2
3 4

BIRDS

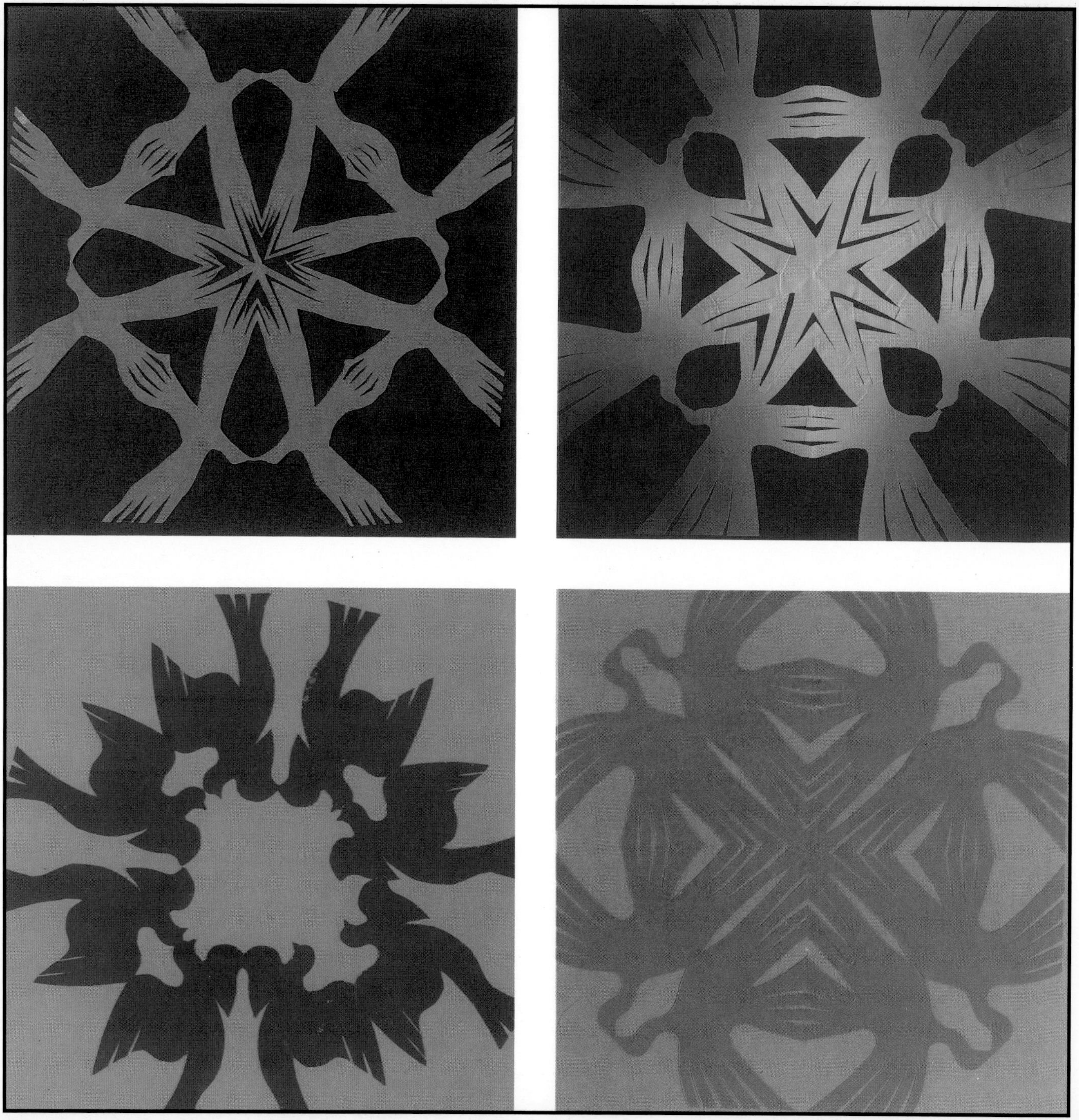

FOLDING STEPS

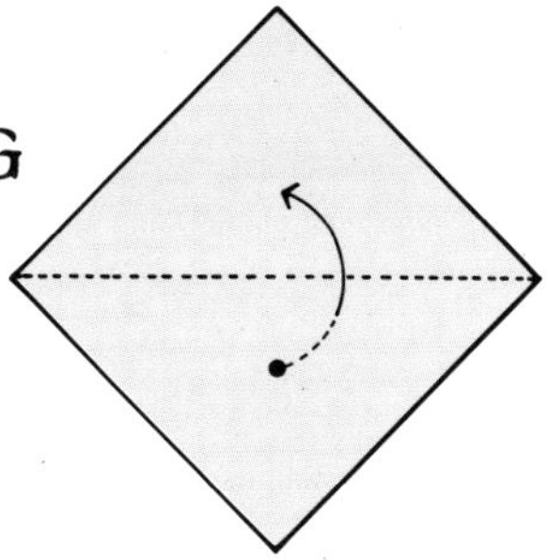

1. Keep color inside and fold paper in half.

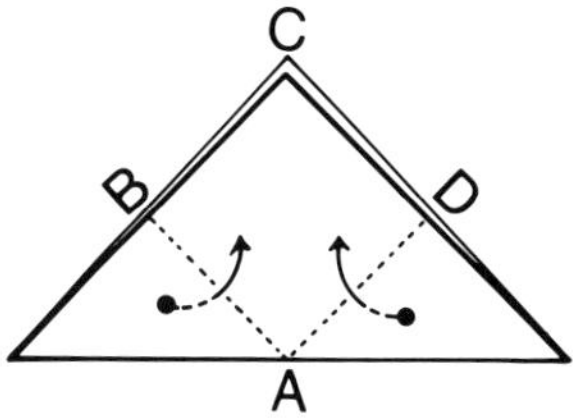

2. Using A,B&D as centers, fold both to C (half fold AB and AD).

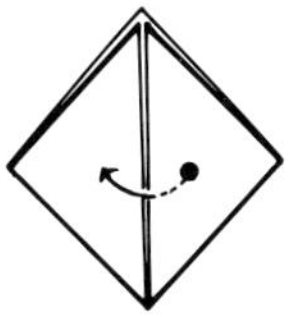

3. Fold in half.

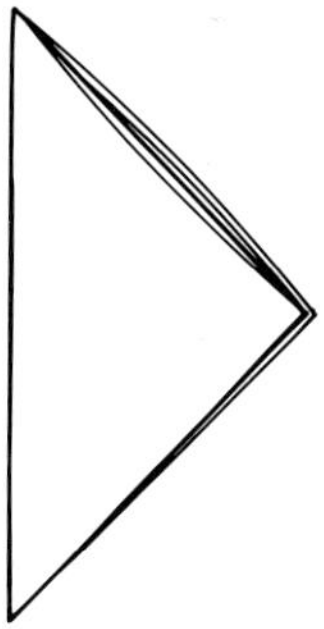

4. Ready for your design or follow pattern below.

PATTERNS

5-¾″ x 5-¾″ Original Size

* Special Pattern Paper

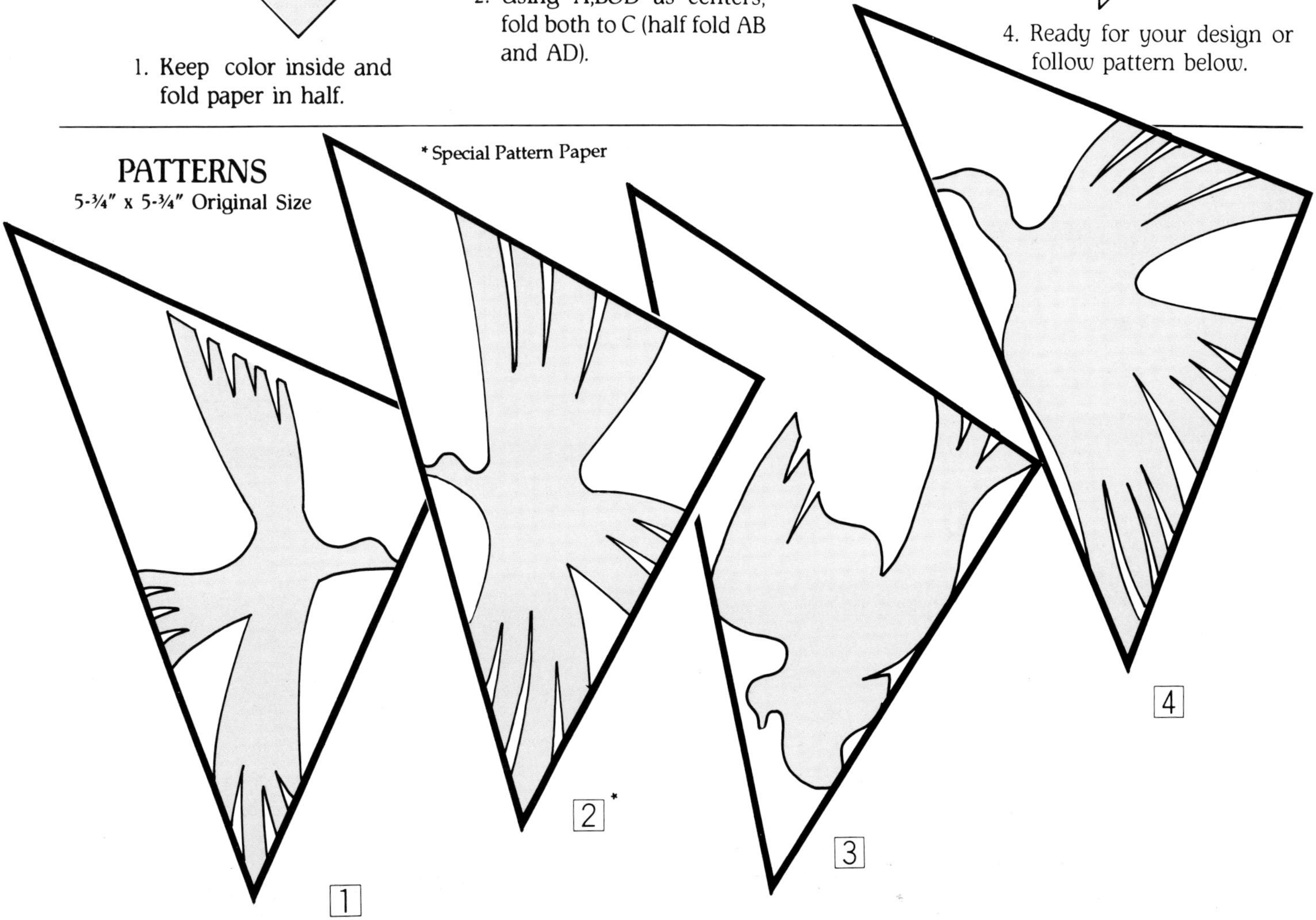

1 2* 3 4

Birds like doves, wild geese, magpies, and the phoenix represent peace, happiness & good fortune.

DOUBLE HAPPINESS

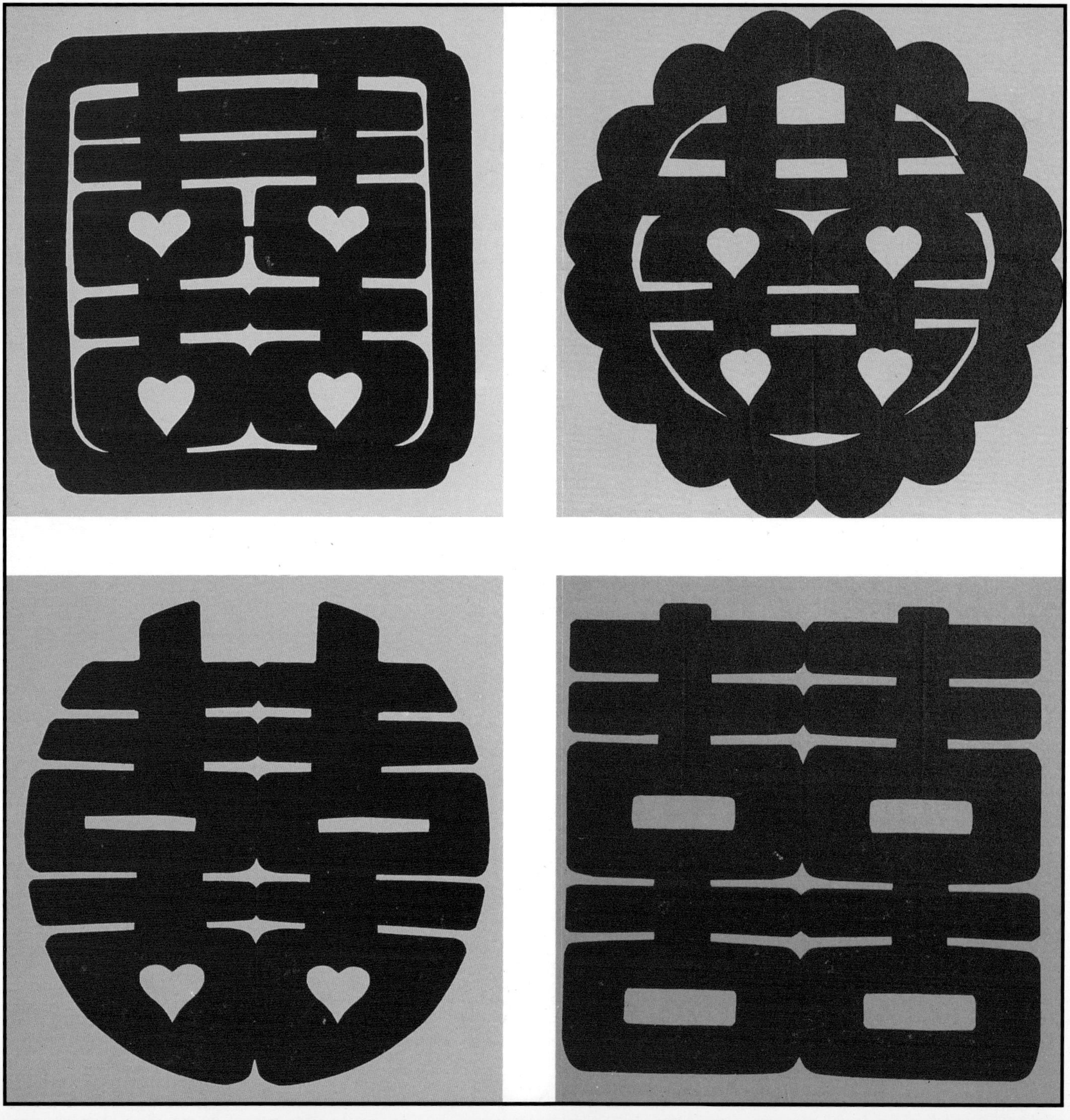

FOLDING STEPS

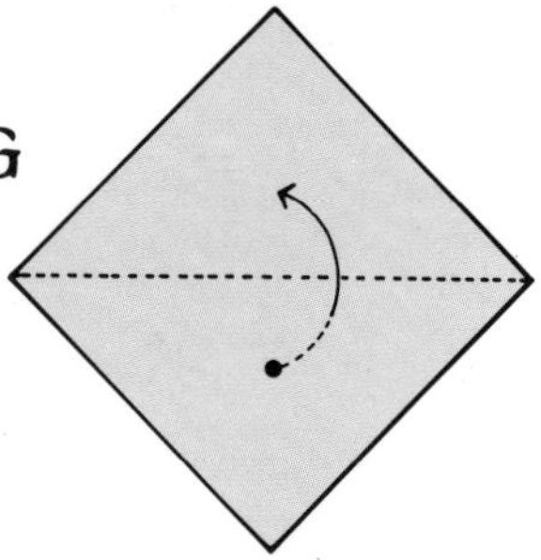

1. Keep color inside and fold paper in half.

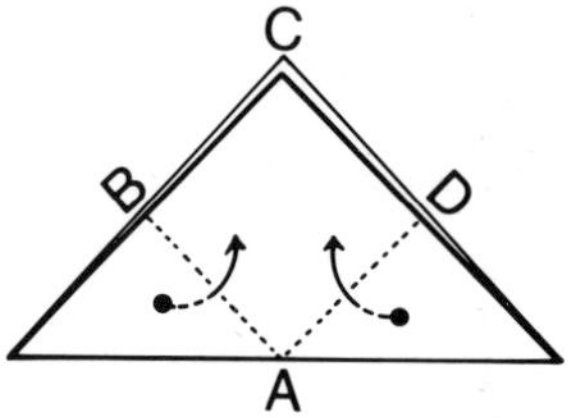

2. Using A,B&D as centers, fold both to C (half fold AB and AD).

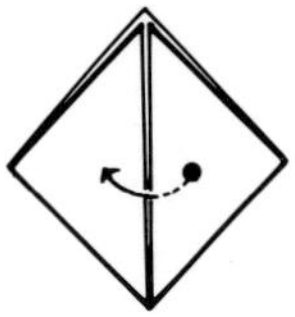

3. Fold in half.

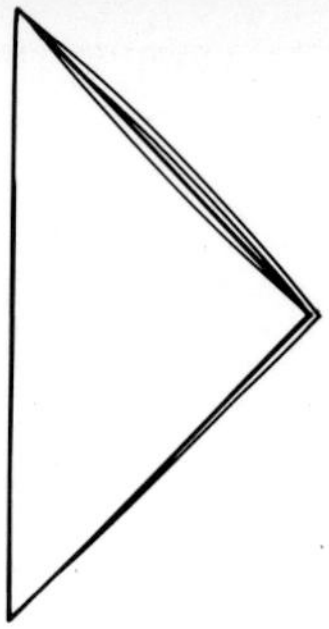

4. Ready for your design or follow pattern below.

PATTERNS

5-¾" x 5-¾" Original Size

* Special Pattern Paper

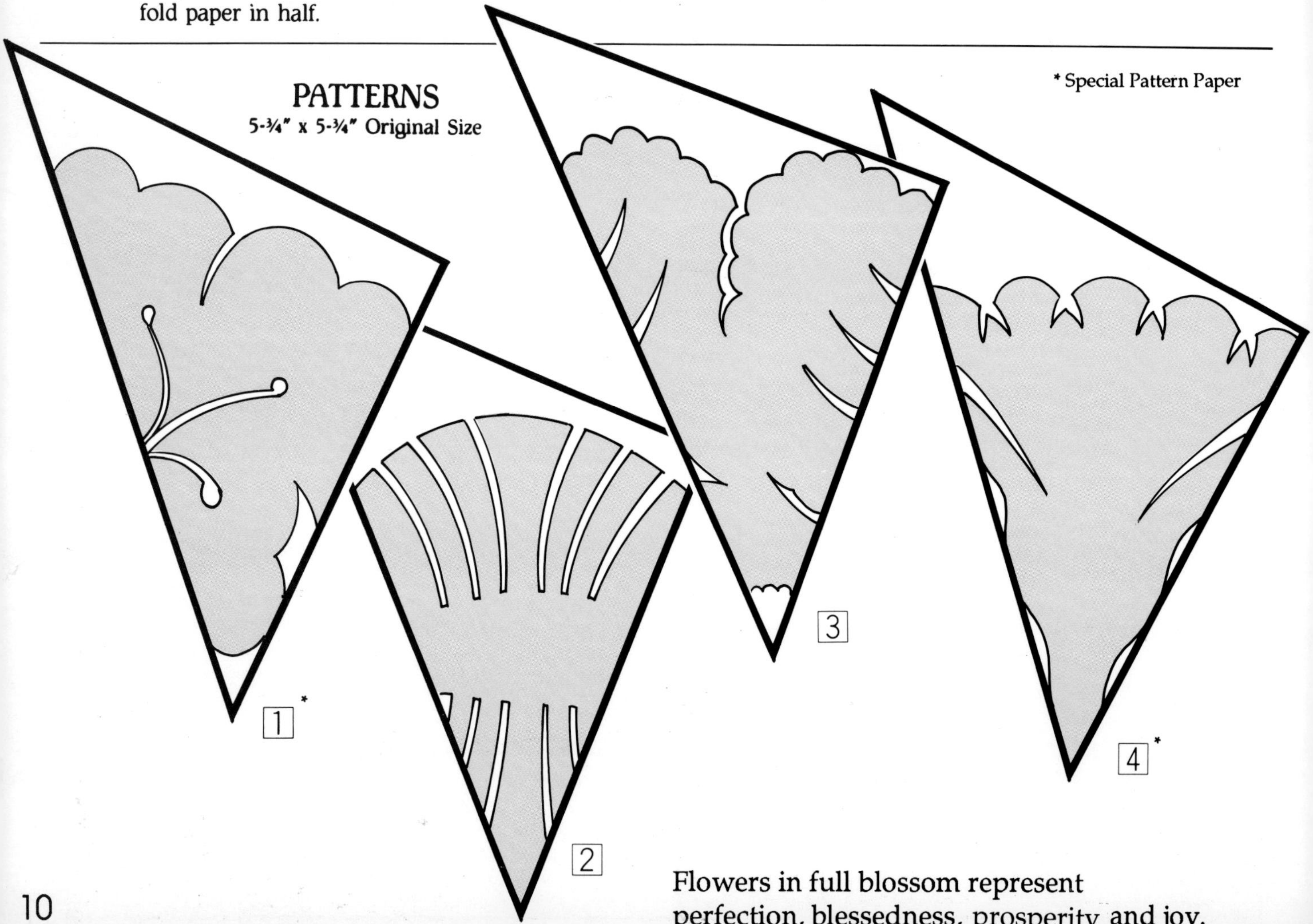

Flowers in full blossom represent perfection, blessedness, prosperity and joy.

1 2
3 4

FLOWERS

FOLDING STEPS

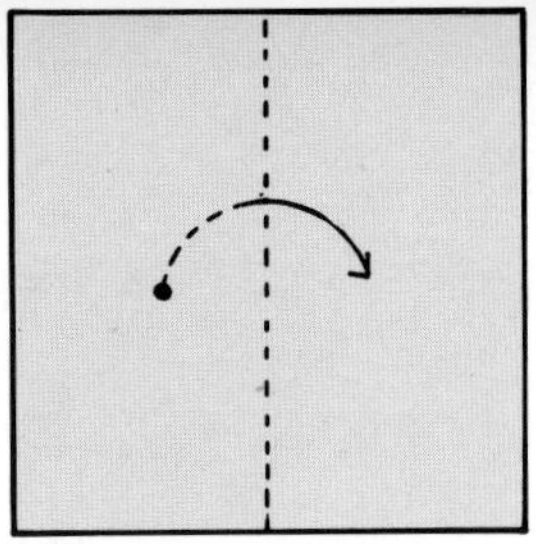

1. Keep color inside and fold in half.

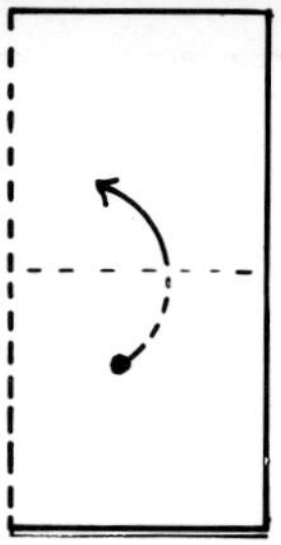

2. Fold in half again.

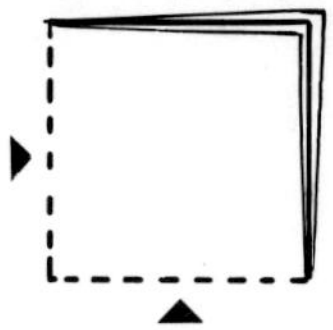

Ready for your own design or follow patterns below.

▶Watch the fold

PATTERNS
(Reduced)

1
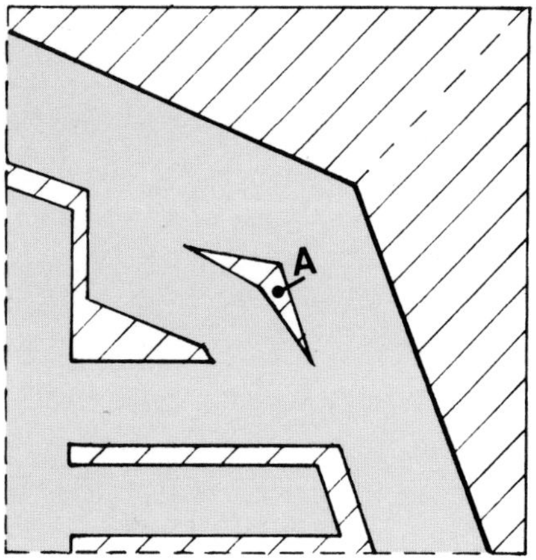

2
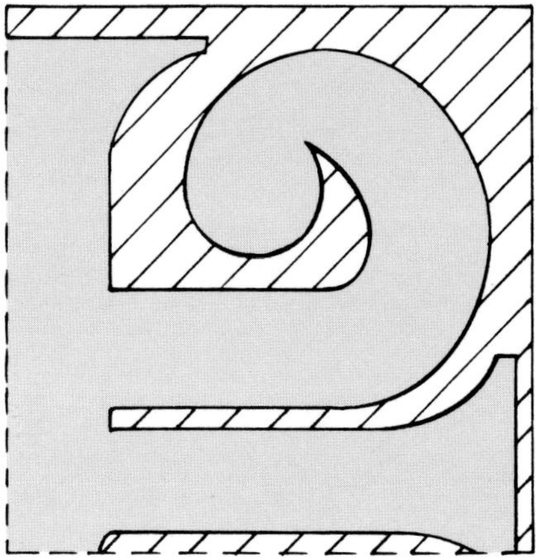

3
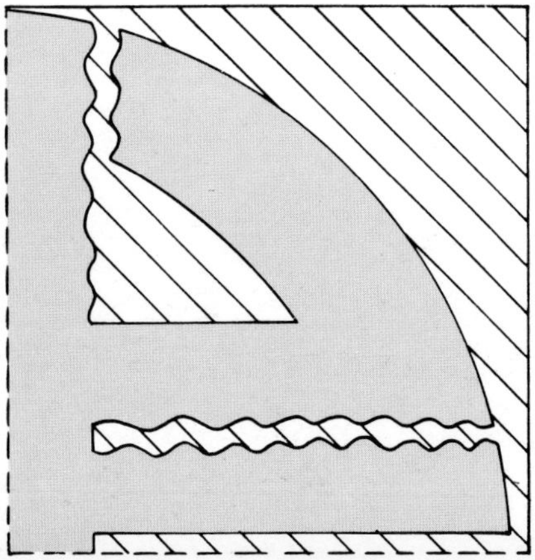

4
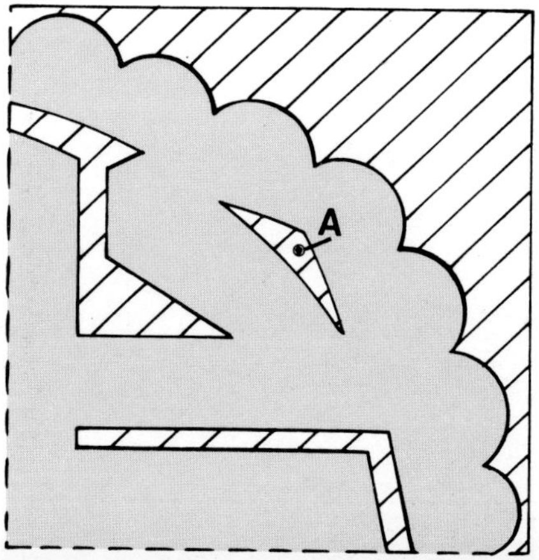

壽

LONGEVITY

The most popular couplet to wish a happy birthday to an elderly person is: "Your good fortune is as immense as the Eastern Sea. Your advanced age is as lofty as the Southern Mountain Range."

A. Using knife to cut out part (A).

1 2
3 4

LONGEVITY

囍 DOUBLE HAPPINESS

The character itself stands for happiness. At a wedding the groom, bride and guests are all joyful. This character wishes the newlyweds " to stick with each other till their hair turns grey" and to "have a harmonious union lasting a hundred years."

FOLDING STEPS

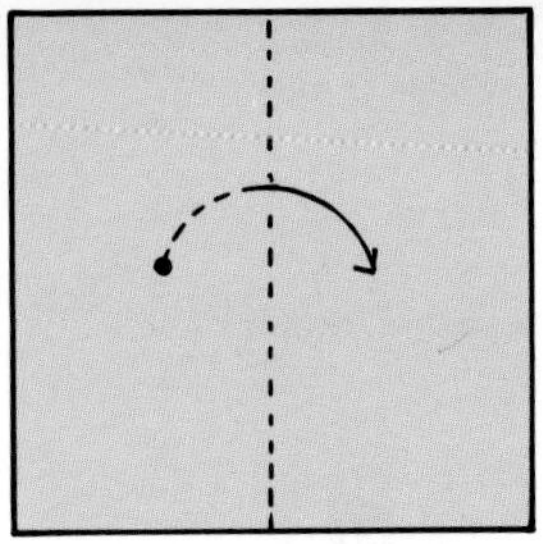

1. Keep the color inside and fold paper in half.

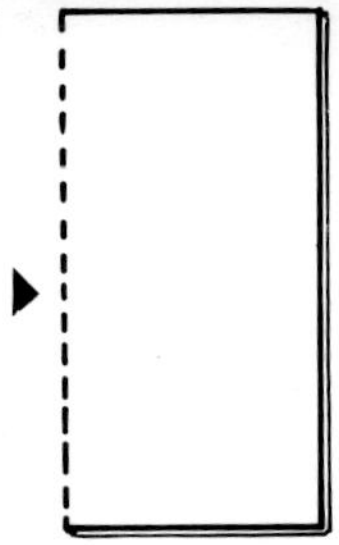

2. Follow the patterns below

PATTERNS

(Reduced)

▶Watch the fold

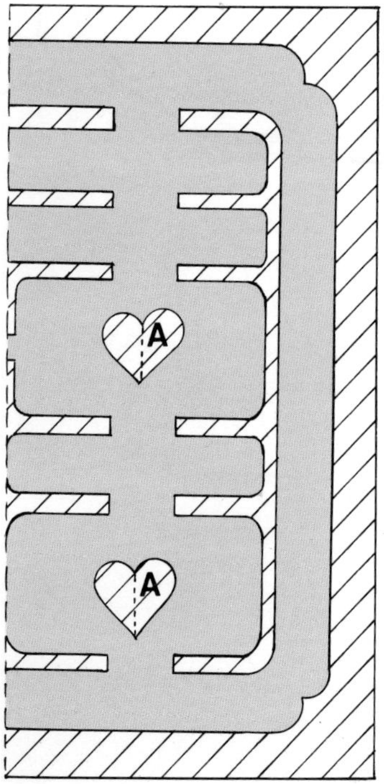

1

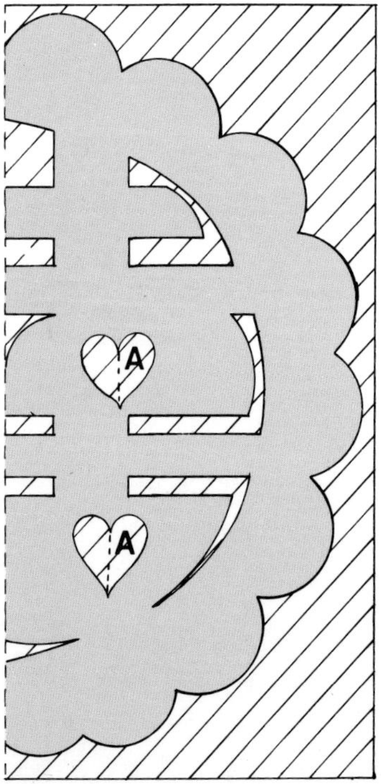

2

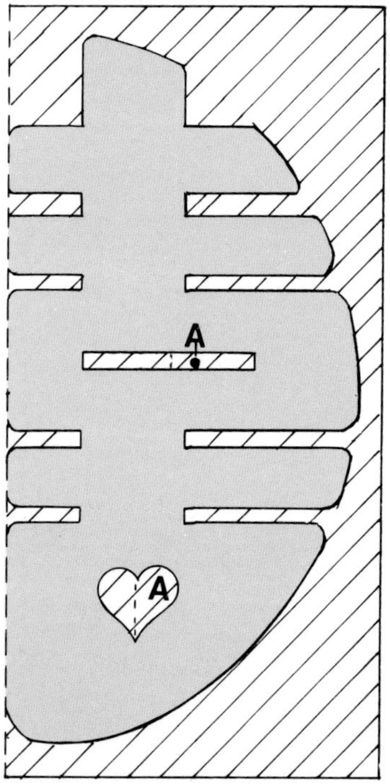

3

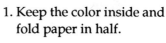

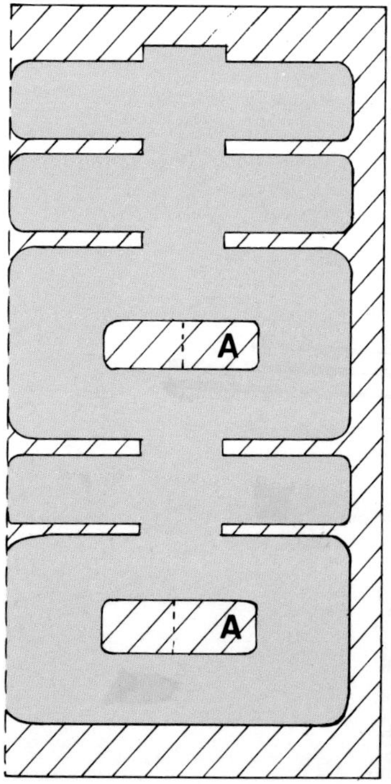

4

A. Use a knife to cut out part (A).